VIOLIN

101 DISNEY SONGS

Available for
FLUTE, CLARINET, ALTO SAX, TENOR SAX, TRUMPET,
HORN, TROMBONE, VIOLA, CELLO

T0079465

ISBN 978-1-5400-0240-2

Disney characters and artwork © Disney

The following songs are the property of:

Bourne Co.
Music Publishers
5 West 37th Street
New York, NY 10018

BABY MINE
GIVE A LITTLE WHISTLE
HEIGH-HO
HI-DIDDLE-DEE-DEE (AN ACTOR'S LIFE FOR ME)
I'M WISHING
I'VE GOT NO STRINGS
SOME DAY MY PRINCE WILL COME
WHEN I SEE AN ELEPHANT FLY
WHEN YOU WISH UPON A STAR
WHISTLE WHILE YOU WORK
WHO'S AFRAID OF THE BIG BAD WOLF?
WITH A SMILE AND A SONG

DISTRIBUTED BY
HAL•LEONARD®
7777 W. BLUEMOUND RD. P.O. BOX 13819 MILWAUKEE, WI 53213

For all works contained herein:
Unauthorized copying, arranging, adapting, recording, Internet posting, public performance, or other distribution of the printed music in this publication is an infringement of copyright. Infringers are liable under the law.

Visit Hal Leonard Online at
www.halleonard.com

CONTENTS

4 Baby Mine
4 The Ballad of Davy Crockett
6 Be Our Guest
7 Beauty and the Beast
5 Bella Notte
8 Belle
12 Best of Friends
9 Bibbidi-Bobbidi-Boo (The Magic Song)
10 Breaking Free
13 Can You Feel the Love Tonight
14 Candle on the Water
15 Chim Chim Cher-ee
16 Circle of Life
17 The Climb
20 Colors of the Wind
18 Cruella De Vil
22 Days in the Sun
21 Do You Want to Build a Snowman?
18 A Dream Is a Wish Your Heart Makes
24 Evermore
19 Feed the Birds (Tuppence a Bag)
26 For the First Time in Forever
28 Friend Like Me
30 Gaston
33 Give a Little Whistle
34 Go the Distance
32 God Help the Outcasts
35 Hakuna Matata
36 Happy Working Song
38 He's a Pirate
39 He's a Tramp
25 Heigh-Ho
27 Hi-Diddle-Dee-Dee (An Actor's Life for Me)
40 How Does a Moment Last Forever
42 How Far I'll Go
41 I Just Can't Wait to Be King
44 I See the Light
46 I'll Make a Man Out of You
43 I'm Late
45 I'm Wishing
48 I've Got a Dream
54 I've Got No Strings
50 If I Can't Love Her
52 If I Never Knew You (End Title)
47 In Summer
54 It's a Small World
55 Kiss the Girl
56 Lava
60 Lavender Blue (Dilly Dilly)
58 Let It Go
61 Let's Go Fly a Kite

62 The Lord Is Good to Me
57 Love Is an Open Door
60 Mickey Mouse March
66 Mother Knows Best
62 My Funny Friend and Me
64 Part of Your World
66 A Pirate's Life
68 Reflection
67 Rumbly in My Tumbly*
69 The Second Star to the Right
70 Seize the Day
74 The Siamese Cat Song
72 So Close
71 So This Is Love
74 Some Day My Prince Will Come
75 Someday
76 Something There
77 A Spoonful of Sugar
78 Supercalifragilisticexpialidocious
80 That's How You Know
79 "This is me."
81 Toyland March
82 Trashin' the Camp (Pop Version)**
84 True Love's Kiss
83 The Unbirthday Song
86 We Belong Together
88 We Know the Way
90 We're All in This Together
85 Westward Ho, the Wagons!
89 A Whale of a Tale
87 When I See an Elephant Fly
92 When She Loved Me
94 When Will My Life Begin?
93 When You Wish Upon a Star
91 Whistle While You Work
96 Who's Afraid of the Big Bad Wolf?
98 A Whole New World
97 Winnie the Pooh*
95 With a Smile and a Song
100 The Wonderful Thing About Tiggers*
102 Written in the Stars
100 Yo Ho (A Pirate's Life for Me)
104 You Are the Music in Me
103 You Can Fly! You Can Fly! You Can Fly!
106 You'll Be in My Heart (Pop Version)**
108 You're Welcome
112 You've Got a Friend in Me
110 Zero to Hero
109 Zip-A-Dee-Doo-Dah
101 Theme from Zorro

*Based on the "Winnie the Pooh" works,
by A. A. Milne and E. H. Shepard

**TARZAN® Owned by Edgar Rice Burroughs, Inc.
and Used by Permission.
© Burroughs/Disney

BABY MINE

from DUMBO

VIOLIN

Copyright © 1941 by Walt Disney Productions
Copyright Renewed
World Rights Controlled by Bourne Co. (ASCAP)
International Copyright Secured All Rights Reserved

Words by NED WASHINGTON
Music by FRANK CHURCHILL

THE BALLAD OF DAVY CROCKETT

from DAVY CROCKETT

© 1954 Wonderland Music Company, Inc. and Walt Disney Music Company
Copyright Renewed.
All Rights Reserved. Used by Permission.

Words by TOM BLACKBURN
Music by GEORGE BRUNS

BELLA NOTTE

from LADY AND THE TRAMP

© 1952 Walt Disney Music Company
Copyright Renewed.
All Rights Reserved. Used by Permission.

Music and Lyrics by PEGGY LEE
and SONNY BURKE

Slowly

VIOLIN

BE OUR GUEST

from BEAUTY AND THE BEAST

© 1991 Wonderland Music Company, Inc. and Walt Disney Music Company
All Rights Reserved. Used by Permission.

Music by ALAN MENKEN
Lyrics by HOWARD ASHMAN

Moderately

BEAUTY AND THE BEAST

VIOLIN

from BEAUTY AND THE BEAST

© 1991 Wonderland Music Company, Inc. and Walt Disney Music Company
All Rights Reserved. Used by Permission.

Music by ALAN MENKEN
Lyrics by HOWARD ASHMAN

Moderately slow

BELLE

from BEAUTY AND THE BEAST

VIOLIN

© 1991 Wonderland Music Company, Inc. and Walt Disney Music Company
All Rights Reserved. Used by Permission.

Music by ALAN MENKEN
Lyrics by HOWARD ASHMAN

BIBBIDI-BOBBIDI-BOO

(The Magic Song)

from CINDERELLA

© 1948 Walt Disney Music Company
Copyright Renewed.
All Rights Reserved. Used by Permission.

Words by JERRY LIVINGSTON
Music by MACK DAVID and AL HOFFMAN

Brightly

VIOLIN

BREAKING FREE

from HIGH SCHOOL MUSICAL

© 2005 Walt Disney Music Company
All Rights Reserved. Used by Permission.

Words and Music by
JAMIE HOUSTON

Moderately

VIOLIN

BEST OF FRIENDS

from THE FOX AND THE HOUND

© 1977 Walt Disney Music Company and Wonderland Music Company, Inc.
Copyright Renewed.
All Rights Reserved. Used by Permission.

Words by STAN FIDEL
Music by RICHARD JOHNSTON

Moderately

CAN YOU FEEL THE LOVE TONIGHT

from THE LION KING

VIOLIN

© 1994 Wonderland Music Company, Inc.
All Rights Reserved. Used by Permission.

Music by ELTON JOHN
Lyrics by TIM RICE

Pop Ballad

VIOLIN

CANDLE ON THE WATER

from PETE'S DRAGON

© 1976 Walt Disney Music Company and Wonderland Music Company, Inc.
Copyright Renewed.
All Rights Reserved. Used by Permission.

Words and Music by AL KASHA
and JOEL HIRSCHHORN

Spiritually

CHIM CHIM CHER-EE

from MARY POPPINS

VIOLIN

© 1963 Wonderland Music Company, Inc.
Copyright Renewed.
All Rights Reserved. Used by Permission.

Words and Music by RICHARD M. SHERMAN
and ROBERT B. SHERMAN

Lightly, with gusto

VIOLIN

CIRCLE OF LIFE

from THE LION KING

© 1994 Wonderland Music Company, Inc.
All Rights Reserved. Used by Permission.

Music by ELTON JOHN
Lyrics by TIM RICE

Moderately (with an African beat)

THE CLIMB

from HANNAH MONTANA: THE MOVIE

IOLIN

2007, 2009 Vistaville Music, Hopeless Rose Music, Music Of Stage Three and Mabe It Big
l Rights for Hopeless Rose Music Administered by Vistaville Music
l Rights for Music Of Stage Three and Mabe it Big Administered by BMG Rights Management (US) LLC
l Rights Reserved. Used by Permission.

Words and Music by JESSI ALEXANDER
and JON MABE

Moderately slow

VIOLIN

CRUELLA DE VIL

from 101 DALMATIANS

© 1961 Walt Disney Music Company
Copyright Renewed.
All Rights Reserved. Used by Permission.

Words and Music b
MEL LEVE

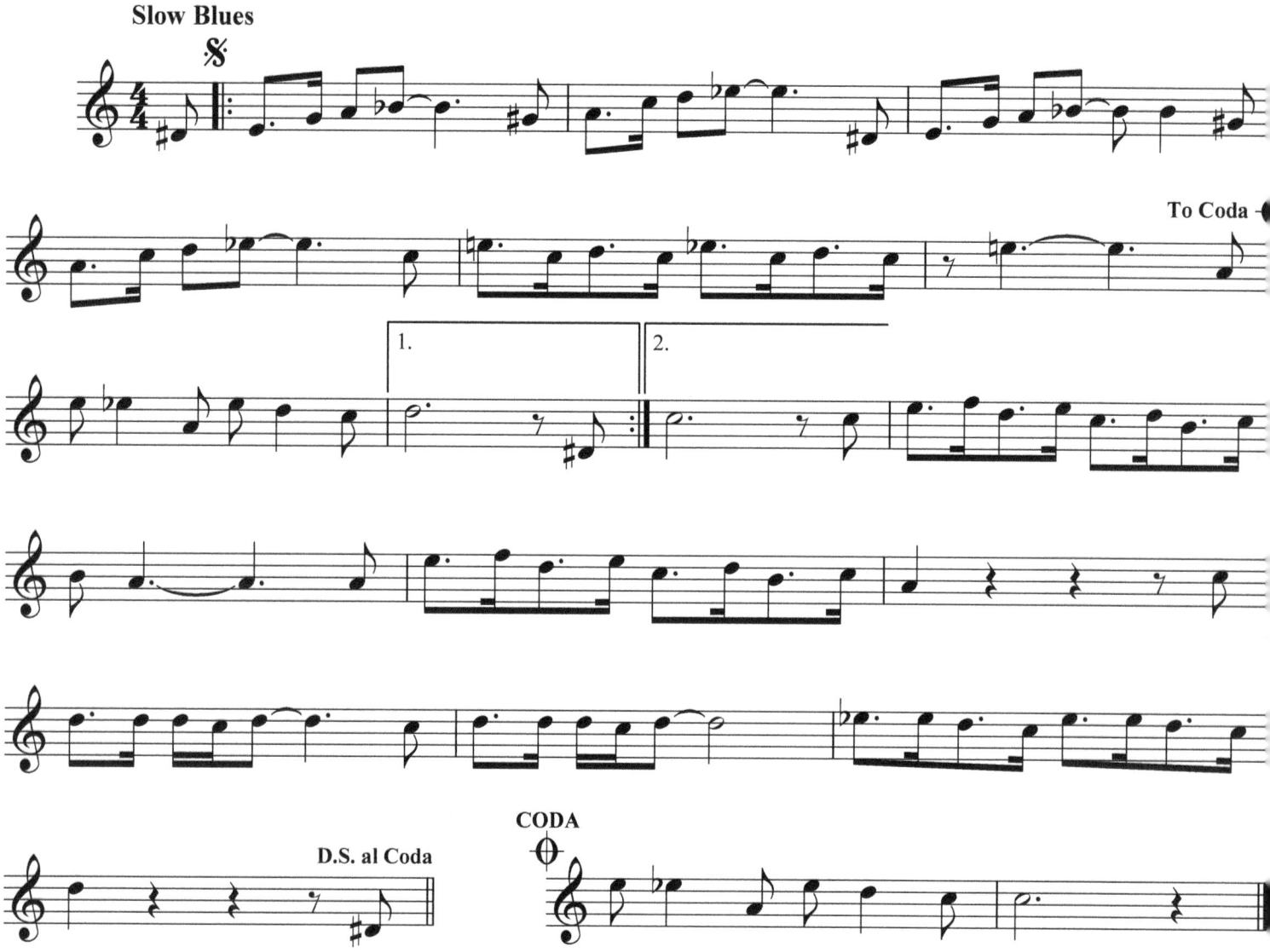

A DREAM IS A WISH YOUR HEART MAKES

from CINDERELLA

© 1948 Walt Disney Music Company
Copyright Renewed.
All Rights Reserved. Used by Permission.

Words and Music by MACK DAVID,
AL HOFFMAN and JERRY LIVINGSTON

FEED THE BIRDS

(Tuppence a Bag)

from MARY POPPINS

© 1963 Wonderland Music Company, Inc.
Copyright Renewed.
All Rights Reserved. Used by Permission.

Words and Music by RICHARD M. SHERMAN
and ROBERT B. SHERMAN

Moderately

VIOLIN

COLORS OF THE WIND

from POCAHONTAS

Music by ALAN MENKEN
Lyrics by STEPHEN SCHWARTZ

© 1995 Wonderland Music Company, Inc. and Walt Disney Music Company
All Rights Reserved. Used by Permission.

DO YOU WANT TO BUILD A SNOWMAN?

from FROZEN

VIOLIN

© 2013 Wonderland Music Company, Inc.
All Rights Reserved. Used by Permission.

Music and Lyrics by KRISTEN ANDERSON-LOPEZ
and ROBERT LOPEZ

DAYS IN THE SUN

from BEAUTY AND THE BEAST

VIOLIN

© 2017 Wonderland Music Company, Inc.
All Rights Reserved. Used by Permission.

Music by ALAN MENKEN
Lyrics by TIM RICE

Slower

EVERMORE

from BEAUTY AND THE BEAST

VIOLIN

© 2017 Wonderland Music Company, Inc.
All Rights Reserved. Used by Permission.

Music by ALAN MENKEN
Lyrics by TIM RICE

HEIGH-HO

(The Dwarfs' Marching Song)

from SNOW WHITE AND THE SEVEN DWARFS

Copyright © 1937 by Bourne Co. (ASCAP)
Copyright Renewed
International Copyright Secured All Rights Reserved

Words by LARRY MOREY
Music by FRANK CHURCHILL

Brightly, cheerfully

FOR THE FIRST TIME IN FOREVER

from FROZEN

VIOLIN

© 2013 Wonderland Music Company, Inc.
All Rights Reserved. Used by Permission.

Music and Lyrics by KRISTEN ANDERSON-LOPEZ
and ROBERT LOPEZ

Moderately, with excitement

Moderately, with expression

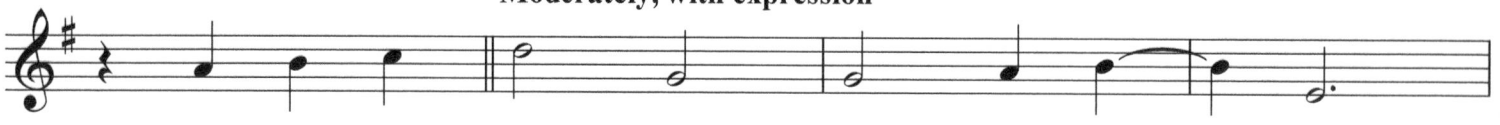

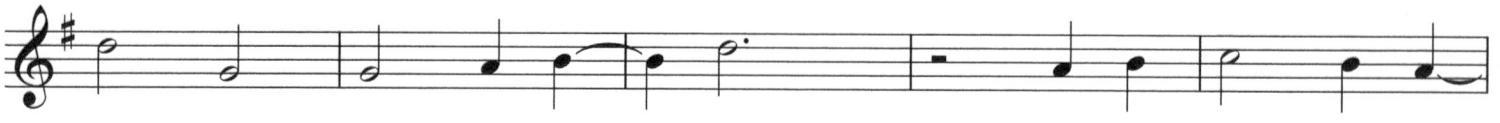

HI-DIDDLE-DEE-DEE

(An Actor's Life for Me)

from PINOCCHIO

Copyright © 1940 by Bourne Co. (ASCAP)
Copyright Renewed
International Copyright Secured All Rights Reserved

Words by NED WASHINGTON
Music by LEIGH HARLINE

VIOLIN

FRIEND LIKE ME

from ALADDIN

© 1992 Wonderland Music Company, Inc. and Walt Disney Music Company
All Rights Reserved. Used by Permission.

Music by ALAN MENKEN
Lyrics by HOWARD ASHMAN

GASTON

from BEAUTY AND THE BEAST

VIOLIN

© 1991 Wonderland Music Company, Inc. and Walt Disney Music Company
All Rights Reserved. Used by Permission.

Music by ALAN MENKEN
Lyrics by HOWARD ASHMAN

Moderately slow, in 1

To Coda
1.
2.
D.S. al Coda
CODA

VIOLIN

GOD HELP THE OUTCASTS

from THE HUNCHBACK OF NOTRE DAME

© 1996 Wonderland Music Company, Inc. and Walt Disney Music Company
All Rights Reserved. Used by Permission.

Music by ALAN MENKEN
Lyrics by STEPHEN SCHWARTZ

GIVE A LITTLE WHISTLE

from PINOCCHIO

Copyright © 1940 by Bourne Co. (ASCAP)
Copyright Renewed
International Copyright Secured All Rights Reserved

Words by NED WASHINGTON
Music by LEIGH HARLINE

Moderately, in 2

VIOLIN

GO THE DISTANCE

from HERCULES

© 1997 Wonderland Music Company, Inc. and Walt Disney Music Company
All Rights Reserved. Used by Permission.

Music by ALAN MENKEN
Lyrics by DAVID ZIPPEL

HAKUNA MATATA

from THE LION KING

VIOLIN

© 1994 Wonderland Music Company, Inc.
All Rights Reserved. Used by Permission.

Music by ELTON JOHN
Lyrics by TIM RICE

HAPPY WORKING SONG

from ENCHANTED

VIOLIN

© 2007 Wonderland Music Company, Inc. and Walt Disney Music Company
All Rights Reserved. Used by Permission.

Music by ALAN MENKEN
Lyrics by STEPHEN SCHWARTZ

D.C. al Coda
CODA

HE'S A PIRATE

from PIRATES OF THE CARIBBEAN: THE CURSE OF THE BLACK PEARL

VIOLIN

© 2003 Walt Disney Music Company
All Rights Reserved. Used by Permission.

Music by KLAUS BADELT,
GEOFFREY ZANELLI and HANS ZIMMER

HE'S A TRAMP

from LADY AND THE TRAMP

© 1952 Walt Disney Music Company
Copyright Renewed.
All Rights Reserved. Used by Permission.

Words and Music by PEGGY LEE
and SONNY BURKE

Moderately

HOW DOES A MOMENT LAST FOREVER

from BEAUTY AND THE BEAST

VIOLIN

© 2017 Wonderland Music Company, Inc.
All Rights Reserved. Used by Permission.

Music by ALAN MENKEN
Lyrics by TIM RICE

Moderately

I JUST CAN'T WAIT TO BE KING

from THE LION KING

VIOLIN

© 1994 Wonderland Music Company, Inc.
All Rights Reserved. Used by Permission.

Music by ELTON JOHN
Lyrics by TIM RICE

HOW FAR I'LL GO

from MOANA

VIOLIN

© 2016 Walt Disney Music Company
All Rights Reserved. Used by Permission.

Music and Lyrics by
LIN-MANUEL MIRANDA

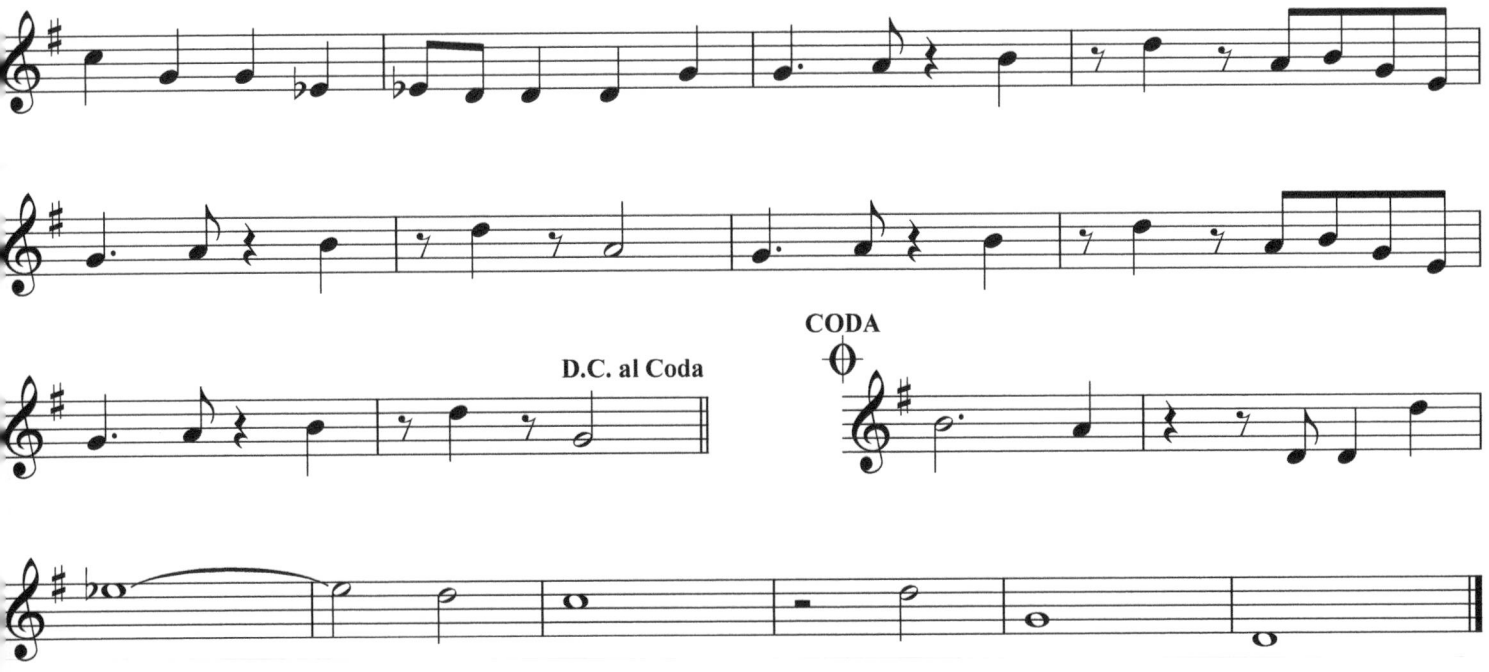

I'M LATE

from ALICE IN WONDERLAND

© 1949 Walt Disney Music Company
Copyright Renewed.
All Rights Reserved. Used by Permission.

Words by BOB HILLIARD
Music by SAMMY FAIN

Moderately fast

I SEE THE LIGHT

from TANGLED

VIOLIN

© 2010 Wonderland Music Company, Inc. and Walt Disney Music Company
All Rights Reserved. Used by Permission.

Music by ALAN MENKEN
Lyrics by GLENN SLATER

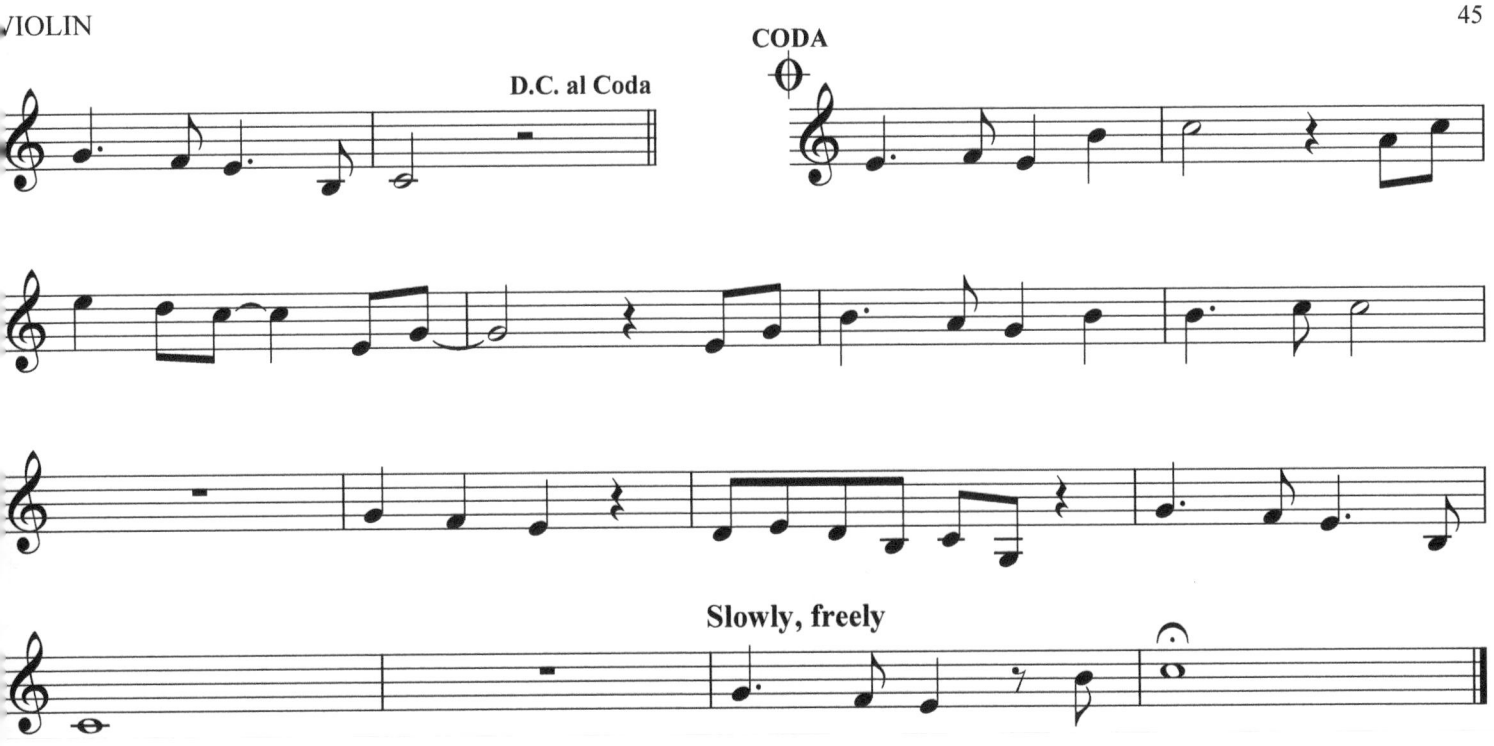

I'M WISHING

from SNOW WHITE AND THE SEVEN DWARFS

Copyright © 1937 by Bourne Co. (ASCAP)
Copyright Renewed
International Copyright Secured All Rights Reserved

Words by LARRY MOREY
Music by FRANK CHURCHILL

I'LL MAKE A MAN OUT OF YOU

from MULAN

VIOLIN

© 1998 Walt Disney Music Company
All Rights Reserved. Used by Permission.

Music by MATTHEW WILDER
Lyrics by DAVID ZIPPEL

IN SUMMER

from FROZEN

VIOLIN

© 2013 Wonderland Music Company, Inc.
All Rights Reserved. Used by Permission.

Music and Lyrics by KRISTEN ANDERSON-LOPEZ
and ROBERT LOPEZ

Moderately, in 2

I'VE GOT A DREAM

from TANGLED

VIOLIN

© 2010 Wonderland Music Company, Inc. and Walt Disney Music Company
All Rights Reserved. Used by Permission.

Music by ALAN MENKEN
Lyrics by GLENN SLATER

Moderately fast

1.
2.
Fine
D.S. al Fine
(take 2nd ending)

IF I CAN'T LOVE HER

from BEAUTY AND THE BEAST: THE BROADWAY MUSICAL

VIOLIN

© 1994 Wonderland Music Company, Inc., Menken Music,
Trunksong Music Ltd. and Walt Disney Music Company
All Rights Reserved. Used by Permission.

Music by ALAN MENKEN
Lyrics by TIM RICE

VIOLIN

IF I NEVER KNEW YOU

(End Title)

from POCAHONTAS

© 1995 Wonderland Music Company, Inc. and Walt Disney Music Company
All Rights Reserved. Used by Permission.

Music by ALAN MENKEN
Lyrics by STEPHEN SCHWARTZ

Moderately slow

I'VE GOT NO STRINGS

from PINOCCHIO

VIOLIN

Copyright © 1940 by Bourne Co. (ASCAP)
Copyright Renewed
International Copyright Secured All Rights Reserved

Words by NED WASHINGTON
Music by LEIGH HARLINE

IT'S A SMALL WORLD

from Disney Parks' "it's a small world" attraction

© 1963 Wonderland Music Company, Inc.
Copyright Renewed.
All Rights Reserved. Used by Permission.

Words and Music by RICHARD M. SHERMAN
and ROBERT B. SHERMAN

KISS THE GIRL

from THE LITTLE MERMAID

VIOLIN

© 1988 Wonderland Music Company, Inc. and Walt Disney Music Company
All Rights Reserved. Used by Permission.

Music by ALAN MENKEN
Lyrics by HOWARD ASHMAN

LAVA

from LAVA

VIOLIN

© 2015 Walt Disney Music Company and Pixar Talking Pictures
All Rights Reserved. Used by Permission.

Music and Lyrics by
JAMES FORD MURPHY

Moderately slow, in 2

LOVE IS AN OPEN DOOR

from FROZEN

IOLIN

2013 Wonderland Music Company, Inc.
l Rights Reserved. Used by Permission.

Music and Lyrics by KRISTEN ANDERSON-LOPEZ
and ROBERT LOPEZ

Moderately

VIOLIN

LET IT GO
from FROZEN

© 2013 Wonderland Music Company, Inc.
All Rights Reserved. Used by Permission.

Music and Lyrics by KRISTEN ANDERSON-LOPE
and ROBERT LOPE

Slowly, in 2

Fine
D.S. al Fine

VIOLIN

LAVENDER BLUE

(Dilly Dilly)

from SO DEAR TO MY HEART

© 1948 Walt Disney Music Company
Copyright Renewed.
All Rights Reserved. Used by Permission.

Words by LARRY MORE
Music by ELIOT DANIE

MICKEY MOUSE MARCH

from THE MICKEY MOUSE CLUB

© 1955 Walt Disney Music Company
Copyright Renewed.
All Rights Reserved. Used by Permission.

Words and Music by
JIMMIE DODI

LET'S GO FLY A KITE

from MARY POPPINS

1963 Wonderland Music Company, Inc.
opyright Renewed.
ll Rights Reserved. Used by Permission.

Words and Music by RICHARD M. SHERMAN
and ROBERT B. SHERMAN

With gusto

VIOLIN

THE LORD IS GOOD TO ME

from MELODY TIME

© 1946 Walt Disney Music Company
Copyright Renewed.
All Rights Reserved. Used by Permission.

Words and Music by KIM GANNO
and WALTER KEN

MY FUNNY FRIEND AND ME

from THE EMPEROR'S NEW GROOVE

© 2000 Wonderland Music Company, Inc.
All Rights Reserved. Used by Permission.

Lyrics by STING
Music by STING and DAVID HARTLE

VIOLIN

PART OF YOUR WORLD

from THE LITTLE MERMAID

© 1988 Wonderland Music Company, Inc. and Walt Disney Music Company
All Rights Reserved. Used by Permission.

Music by ALAN MENKEN
Lyrics by HOWARD ASHMAN

Moderately bright

MOTHER KNOWS BEST

from TANGLED

VIOLIN

© 2010 Wonderland Music Company, Inc. and Walt Disney Music Company
All Rights Reserved. Used by Permission.

Music by ALAN MENKEI
Lyrics by GLENN SLATE

Moderately slow, in 2

A PIRATE'S LIFE

from PETER PAN

© 1951 Walt Disney Music Company
Copyright Renewed.
All Rights Reserved. Used by Permission.

Words by ED PENNER
Music by OLIVER WALLACI

Moderately, with a bounce

RUMBLY IN MY TUMBLY

from THE MANY ADVENTURES OF WINNIE THE POOH

© 1964 Wonderland Music Company, Inc.
Copyright Renewed.
All Rights Reserved. Used by Permission.

Words and Music by RICHARD M. SHERMAN
and ROBERT B. SHERMAN

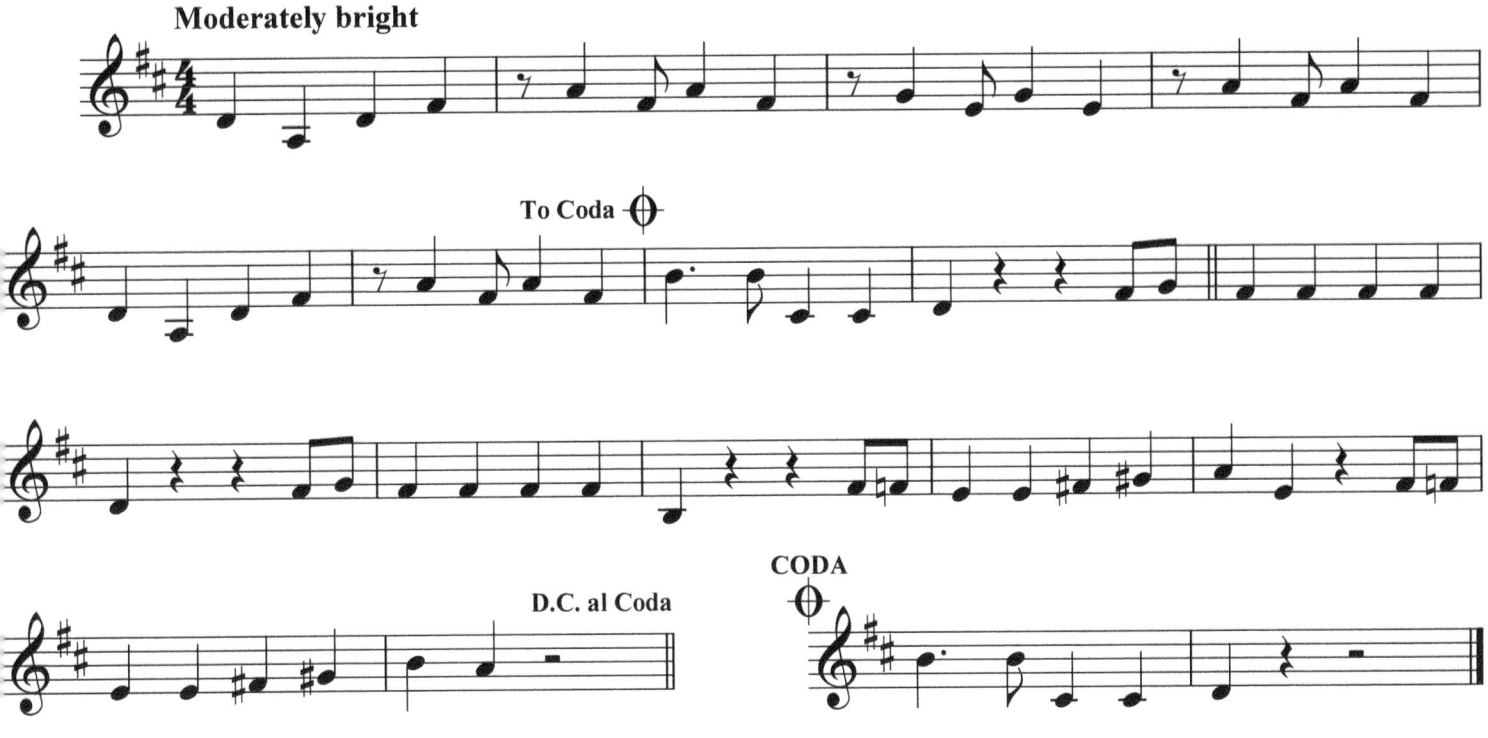

VIOLIN

REFLECTION
from MULAN

© 1998 Walt Disney Music Company
All Rights Reserved. Used by Permission.

Music by MATTHEW WILDE
Lyrics by DAVID ZIPPE

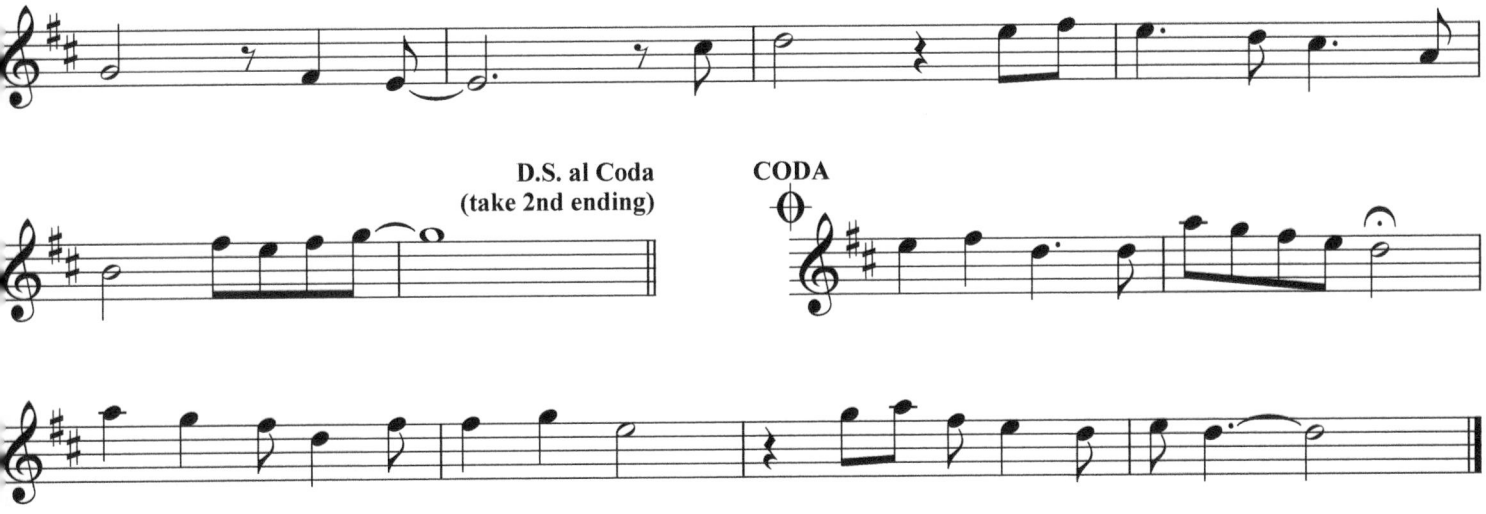

THE SECOND STAR TO THE RIGHT

from PETER PAN

© 1951 Walt Disney Music Company
Copyright Renewed.
All Rights Reserved. Used by Permission.

Words by SAMMY CAHN
Music by SAMMY FAIN

SEIZE THE DAY

from NEWSIES

VIOLIN

© 1992 Wonderland Music Company, Inc. obo Itself, Trunksong Music LTD. and Menken Music
All Rights Reserved. Used by Permission.

Music by ALAN MENKEN
Lyrics by JACK FELDMAN

SO THIS IS LOVE

from CINDERELLA

OLIN

1948 Walt Disney Music Company
pyright Renewed.
Rights Reserved. Used by Permission.

Words and Music by AL HOFFMAN,
MACK DAVID and JERRY LIVINGSTON

SO CLOSE

from ENCHANTED

VIOLIN

© 2007 Wonderland Music Company, Inc. and Walt Disney Music Company
All Rights Reserved. Used by Permission.

Music by ALAN MENKE
Lyrics by STEPHEN SCHWART

Moderately slow, in 4

Slowly, freely

VIOLIN

THE SIAMESE CAT SONG

from LADY AND THE TRAMP

© 1953 Walt Disney Music Company
Copyright Renewed.
All Rights Reserved. Used by Permission.

Words and Music by PEGGY LE
and SONNY BURK

SOME DAY MY PRINCE WILL COME

from SNOW WHITE AND THE SEVEN DWARFS

Copyright © 1937 by Bourne Co. (ASCAP)
Copyright Renewed
International Copyright Secured All Rights Reserved

Words by LARRY MORE
Music by FRANK CHURCHIL

SOMEDAY

from THE HUNCHBACK OF NOTRE DAME

OLIN

1996 Wonderland Music Company, Inc. and Walt Disney Music Company
Rights Reserved. Used by Permission.

Music by ALAN MENKEN
Lyrics by STEPHEN SCHWARTZ

SOMETHING THERE

from BEAUTY AND THE BEAST

VIOLIN

© 1991 Wonderland Music Company, Inc. and Walt Disney Music Company
All Rights Reserved. Used by Permission.

Music by ALAN MENKE
Lyrics by HOWARD ASHMA

A SPOONFUL OF SUGAR

from MARY POPPINS

OLIN

963 Wonderland Music Company, Inc.
pyright Renewed.
Rights Reserved. Used by Permission.

Words and Music by RICHARD M. SHERMAN
and ROBERT B. SHERMAN

SUPERCALIFRAGILISTICEXPIALIDOCIOUS

VIOLIN

from MARY POPPINS

© 1963 Wonderland Music Company, Inc.
Copyright Renewed.
All Rights Reserved. Used by Permission.

Words and Music by RICHARD M. SHERMA
and ROBERT B. SHERMA

Brightly

"THIS IS ME."

from RATATOUILLE

OLIN

2007 Walt Disney Music Company and Pixar Talking Pictures
ministered by Walt Disney Music Company
Rights Reserved. Used by Permission.

Music by MICHAEL GIACCHINO

THAT'S HOW YOU KNOW

from ENCHANTED

VIOLIN

© 2007 Wonderland Music Company, Inc. and Walt Disney Music Company
All Rights Reserved. Used by Permission.

Music by ALAN MENKE
Lyrics by STEPHEN SCHWARTZ

TOYLAND MARCH

from BABES IN TOYLAND

1961 Walt Disney Music Company
pyright Renewed.
l Rights Reserved. Used by Permission.

Adapted from V. HERBERT Melody
Words by MEL LEVEN
Music by GEORGE BRUNS

March tempo

TRASHIN' THE CAMP

(Pop Version)

from TARZAN™

VIOLIN

© 1999 Edgar Rice Burroughs, Inc. and Walt Disney Music Company
All Rights Reserved. Used by Permission.
TARZAN® Owned by Edgar Rice Burroughs, Inc. and Used by Permission.
© Burroughs/Disney

Words and Music b
PHIL COLLIN

THE UNBIRTHDAY SONG

from ALICE IN WONDERLAND

OLIN

948 Walt Disney Music Company
pyright Renewed.
Rights Reserved. Used by Permission.

Words and Music by MACK DAVID,
AL HOFFMAN and JERRY LIVINGSTON

TRUE LOVE'S KISS

from ENCHANTED

VIOLIN

© 2007 Wonderland Music Company, Inc. and Walt Disney Music Company
All Rights Reserved. Used by Permission.

Music by ALAN MENKE
Lyrics by STEPHEN SCHWART

WESTWARD HO, THE WAGONS!

from WESTWARD HO, THE WAGONS!

1955 Wonderland Music Company, Inc. and Walt Disney Music Company
opyright Renewed.
ll Rights Reserved. Used by Permission.

Words by TOM BLACKBURN
Music by GEORGE BRUNS

WE BELONG TOGETHER

from TOY STORY 3

VIOLIN

© 2010 Walt Disney Music Company and Pixar Talking Pictures
All Rights Reserved. Used by Permission.

Music and Lyrics b
RANDY NEWMA

WHEN I SEE AN ELEPHANT FLY

from DUMBO

opyright © 1941 by Walt Disney Productions
opyright Renewed
orld Rights Controlled by Bourne Co. (ASCAP)
ternational Copyright Secured All Rights Reserved

Words by NED WASHINGTON
Music by OLIVER WALLACE

Moderately fast (♩♩ = ♩♪)

WE KNOW THE WAY

from MOANA

VIOLIN

© 2016 Walt Disney Music Company
All Rights Reserved. Used by Permission.

Music by OPETAIA FOA
Lyrics by OPETAIA FOA
and LIN-MANUEL MIRANDA

Moderately

A WHALE OF A TALE

from 20,000 LEAGUES UNDER THE SEA

OLIN

1953 Wonderland Music Company, Inc.
pyright Renewed.
Rights Reserved. Used by Permission.

Words and Music by NORMAN GIMBEL
and AL HOFFMAN

VIOLIN

WE'RE ALL IN THIS TOGETHER

from HIGH SCHOOL MUSICAL

© 2005 Walt Disney Music Company
All Rights Reserved. Used by Permission.

Words and Music by MATTHEW GERRAR
and ROBBIE NEV

WHISTLE WHILE YOU WORK

from SNOW WHITE AND THE SEVEN DWARFS

opyright © 1937 by Bourne Co. (ASCAP)
opyright Renewed
ternational Copyright Secured All Rights Reserved

Words by LARRY MOREY
Music by FRANK CHURCHILL

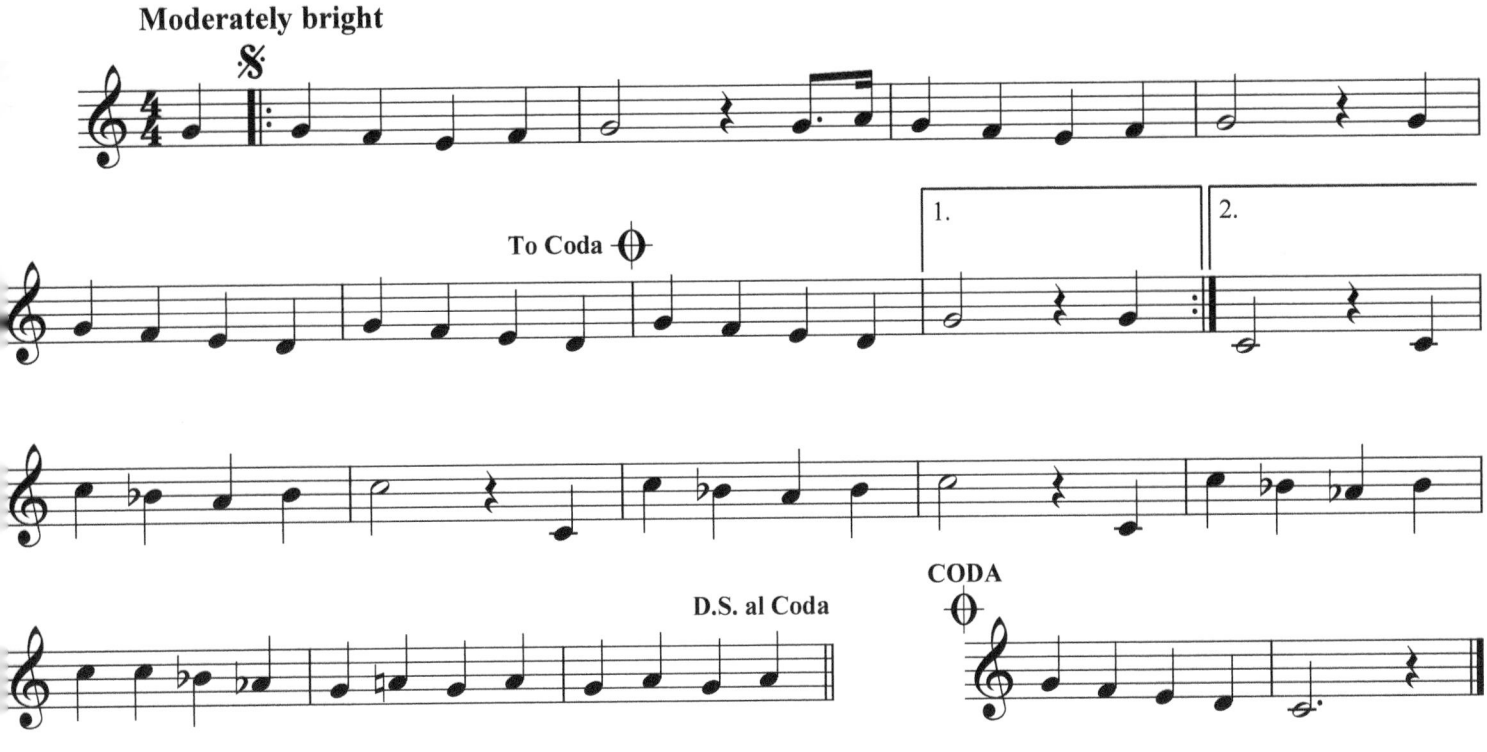

VIOLIN

WHEN SHE LOVED ME

from TOY STORY 2

© 1999 Walt Disney Music Company and Pixar Talking Pictures
All Rights Reserved. Used by Permission.

Music and Lyrics
RANDY NEWMA

WHEN YOU WISH UPON A STAR

from PINOCCHIO

IOLIN

pyright © 1940 by Bourne Co. (ASCAP)
pyright Renewed
ternational Copyright Secured All Rights Reserved

Words by NED WASHINGTON
Music by LEIGH HARLINE

WHEN WILL MY LIFE BEGIN?

from TANGLED

VIOLIN

© 2010 Wonderland Music Company, Inc. and Walt Disney Music Company
All Rights Reserved. Used by Permission.

Music by ALAN MENKEN
Lyrics by GLENN SLATER

WITH A SMILE AND A SONG

from SNOW WHITE AND THE SEVEN DWARFS

Copyright © 1937 by Bourne Co. (ASCAP)
Copyright Renewed
International Copyright Secured All Rights Reserved

Words by LARRY MOREY
Music by FRANK CHURCHILL

WHO'S AFRAID OF THE BIG BAD WOLF?

from THREE LITTLE PIGS

VIOLIN

Copyright © 1933 by Bourne Co. (ASCAP)
Copyright Renewed
International Copyright Secured All Rights Reserved

Words and Music b
FRANK CHURCHIL
Additional Lyric by ANN RONEL

Moderately, in 2

WINNIE THE POOH

from THE MANY ADVENTURES OF WINNIE THE POOH

OLIN

963 Wonderland Music Company, Inc.
pyright Renewed.
Rights Reserved. Used by Permission.

Words and Music by RICHARD M. SHERMAN
and ROBERT B. SHERMAN

Tenderly

VIOLIN

A WHOLE NEW WORLD

from ALADDIN

© 1992 Wonderland Music Company, Inc. and Walt Disney Music Company
All Rights Reserved. Used by Permission.

Music by ALAN MENKE
Lyrics by TIM RIC

THE WONDERFUL THING ABOUT TIGGERS

VIOLIN

from THE MANY ADVENTURES OF WINNIE THE POOH

© 1964 Wonderland Music Company, Inc.
Copyright Renewed.
All Rights Reserved. Used by Permission.

Words and Music by RICHARD M. SHERMA
and ROBERT B. SHERMA

YO HO

(A Pirate's Life for Me)

from Disney Parks' Pirates of the Caribbean attraction

© 1967 Walt Disney Music Company
Copyright Renewed.
All Rights Reserved. Used by Permission.

Words by XAVIER ATENCI(
Music by GEORGE BRUN

THEME FROM ZORRO

from the Television Series

1966 Walt Disney Music Company
opyright Renewed.
l Rights Reserved. Used by Permission.

Words by NORMAN FOSTER
Music by GEORGE BRUNS

Moderately, in 2

VIOLIN

WRITTEN IN THE STARS

from AIDA

© 1998 Wonderland Music Company, Inc., Happenstance Ltd. and Evadon Ltd.
All Rights Reserved. Used by Permission.

Music by ELTON JOH
Lyrics by TIM RIC

YOU CAN FLY! YOU CAN FLY! YOU CAN FLY!

OLIN

from PETER PAN

1951 Walt Disney Music Company
pyright Renewed.
Rights Reserved. Used by Permission.

Words by SAMMY CAHN
Music by SAMMY FAIN

VIOLIN

YOU ARE THE MUSIC IN ME

from HIGH SCHOOL MUSICAL 2

© 2007 Walt Disney Music Company
All Rights Reserved. Used by Permission.

Words and Music b
JAMIE HOUSTO

Moderately fast Rock

VIOLIN

YOU'LL BE IN MY HEART

(Pop Version)

from TARZAN™

© 1999 Edgar Rice Burroughs, Inc. and Walt Disney Music Company
All Rights Reserved. Used by Permission.
TARZAN® Owned by Edgar Rice Burroughs, Inc. and Used by Permission.
© Burroughs/Disney

Words and Music
PHIL COLLIN

CODA
1.
2.
3
3

YOU'RE WELCOME

from MOANA

VIOLIN

© 2016 Walt Disney Music Company
All Rights Reserved. Used by Permission.

Music and Lyrics
LIN-MANUEL MIRANDA

ZIP-A-DEE-DOO-DAH

from SONG OF THE SOUTH

1945 Walt Disney Music Company
pyright Renewed.
l Rights Reserved. Used by Permission.

Words by RAY GILBERT
Music by ALLIE WRUBEL

Brightly

VIOLIN

ZERO TO HERO

from HERCULES

© 1997 Wonderland Music Company, Inc. and Walt Disney Music Company
All Rights Reserved. Used by Permission.

Music by ALAN MENKE
Lyrics by DAVID ZIPPE

D.C. al Coda
CODA

YOU'VE GOT A FRIEND IN ME

from TOY STORY

VIOLIN

© 1995 Walt Disney Music Company
All Rights Reserved. Used by Permission.

Music and Lyrics
RANDY NEWMAN